# Weight Loss Smoot

## 95 Delicious Smoothie Recipes

### By

## Liana Green

www.LianasKitchen.co.uk

# DISCLAIMER

This book is not intended as a substitute for the medical advice of physicians. The reader should regularly consult a physician in matters relating to his/her health and particularly with respect to any symptoms that may require diagnosis or medical attention. Although the author and publisher have made every effort to ensure that the information in this book was correct at press time, the author and publisher do not assume and hereby disclaim any liability to any part for any loss, damage, or disruption caused by errors or omissions, whether such errors or omissions result from negligence, accident or any other cause.

# Welcome

Thank you for reading my book, Weight Loss Smoothies. As with my other recipe books I have spent a considerable time researching and developing my smoothie recipes. I hope you enjoy them!

If you have any suggestions or questions please get in touch with me at liana@lianaskitchen.co.uk. I always answer each and every email – in fact, I love hearing from my readers!

If you are interested in other recipes, reviews and tips please head over to www.lianaskitchen.co.uk

You can also join my newsletter where I will let you know as soon as a new book is released – and when they are free or discounted. You will also get to hear about competitions, new recipes and any other exciting news. Just head here and join up http://www.lianaskitchen.co.uk/vip/

# Making Smoothies

Making and consuming smoothies is an excellent way of ensuring your body receives all the nutrients it requires to operate at optimum health levels.

Although smoothies are both tasty and vitamin rich, if you are trying to lose weight it is useful to know how many calories you are taking in each day. Some smoothies can really bump up the calories.

I quite like to start my day with a filling, yet healthy smoothie. Depending on my schedule, or how I am feeling, I might choose a low calorie smoothie to go alongside a bowl of cereal. Or, I might replace my breakfast altogether with a smoothie. If I am just consuming a smoothie for a meal it is important that I choose one that will slowly release energy, perhaps including some oats, seeds or nuts.

## Using This Book

I have split out the 95 smoothie recipes between those under 300 calories, 200 calories and 100 calories. Each smoothie can be had at any time of the day. Some are obviously sweeter than others so you may prefer to save these for an after dinner treat.

Each smoothie recipe is measured out to be a single serving. Of course if you want to make more servings just adjust the recipes accordingly.

The amount of calories per serving, together with the main health benefits of each smoothie, are listed under each recipe.

This smoothie recipe book does not contain a diet plan. I like the flexibility of having a low calorie smoothie either instead of a meal or alongside a healthy meal.

### What makes a healthy meal?

The world is full of every kind of diet and healthy meal idea. I like to keep things simple – keep your food clean. What do I mean by this? Go for unprocessed and as close to nature as possible. The less it has been interfered with by humans the better it is.

If you are interested in any of the clean eating recipes that I use myself, let me know at liana@lianaskitchen.co.uk and I'll get some published on www.lianaskitchen.co.uk

I'm also a strong believer in keeping it realistic. If you have a sweet tooth and enjoy the pleasures of 'treats' or 'desserts' then have them. And they don't have to be full of refined sugars and unhealthy fats. You can get the satisfaction of a tasty treat without consuming any of the bad stuff.

## Which Blender?

The recipes in this book can be made in any good quality blender. For the best results I highly recommend using a high speed blender such as a Nutribullet, Nutri Ninja, Vitamix or Magimix.

For a great budget buy I would suggest looking at the Breville Blend Active. You should be aware that the power of this blender is lower than the high speed blenders mentioned above and you may have to alter the recipes to include more liquid and blend for longer.

I currently use a Nutri Ninja (BL450) and sometimes the Breville Blend Active. They both work well with these smoothie recipes but as the Nutri Ninja has a more powerful motor it copes with the blending process with more ease.

For a full and in depth analysis to smoothie makers head over to my blog where I've put together a handy guide www.lianaskitchen.co.uk/smoothie-makers

## The Ingredients

All the recipes contain ingredients that can be easily found and purchased in your local supermarket or health shop. The idea is to keep things as simple as possible.

**Frozen**

I like to keep some ingredients in the freezer. You can either freeze fresh produce as you purchase it, or buy ready prepared frozen ingredients. More and more supermarkets are catering for the smoothie market by providing items such as frozen mango & pineapple chunks, frozen berries and recently frozen avocado halves. No more waiting for your avocado to get to the perfect ripeness! By using frozen ingredients in your smoothie you also remove the need to add ice cubes.

Remember the more frozen ingredients you add to your smoothie the thicker it will be. You may need to add more liquid to get it moving in your blender.

## Healthy Fats

Healthy fats are essential for good health. Fortunately they are easy to include in a smoothie. Fats can be converted into energy and are necessary for brain development, nerve function and building new cells.

Omega-3 and omega-6 fats cannot be made by the body and need to come from diet alone. Simply add seeds such as pumpkin, soya or flax to your smoothie. Walnuts are another great source.

## Proteins

Protein is a vital requirement in your daily diet, essential for growth, maintenance and repair.

Amino acids are the building blocks that form protein. There are over 20 different kinds of amino acids, 8 essential ones for adults and an additional 2 for children. Your body is unable to make these essential amino acids and so you must obtain them from your diet.

Good sources of protein suitable for smoothies include nuts (particularly brazil and peanuts), milk, soy milk, oats, kale, dried apricots, seeds (pumpkin, flax, chia), Greek yoghurt and cacao.

## Liquid

All smoothie recipes require some liquid to blend the ingredients together. I tend to choose from water, juice (but only freshly squeezed), coconut water, unsweetened almond milk, soy milk or skimmed milk. If any of the smoothie recipes are too thick for you simply add more liquid and blend again. If there are any from the recipes that you are not keen on, or unable to consume, just substitute it for another one.


**Greens**


Green smoothies are a popular weight loss smoothie. They are often a powerhouse of vitamins and nutrients. Make sure you vary up the greens you use each time. This is because most greens contain very small amounts of alkaloids and oxalates. They are not harmful and won't produce any negative symptoms, unless you are consuming the same plant every single day. Also, by rotating your greens you are getting a wider variety of nutrients and keeping it interesting for your taste buds.


I tend to rotate between spinach, kale and Romaine lettuce because I can easily buy them. You can also use Swiss chard, beetroot greens or carrot tops.


**TIP:** When blending greens I always blend up the greens and liquid on their own first. This allows the fibres in the greens to blend effectively and will result in a smoother smoothie. It will also give you more room in your blender cup/jug to add the other ingredients without going over the MAX line.


Not all the recipes in this book are green smoothies. It is important to vary up your smoothies and keep it interesting. Why not indulge in the odd chocolate infused smoothie and treat yourself without the calorie guilt?!


**Organic**

Buy organic when possible. When you can't make sure you peel hard fruits and vegetables or scrub thoroughly before blending. Remove the skins from citrus fruits if they have been waxed.

## Storing Your Smoothies

Smoothies are always best when consumed straight away, making them as fresh as possible. However, this isn't always practical so you may need to make them in advance. Smoothies can be frozen or kept in a sealed container in the fridge. Just make sure you shake well before drinking as the smoothie may have separated.

# Conversion

**VOLUME**

| ML | FL OZ | CUP |
|---|---|---|
| 250 | 8 | 1 |
| 180 | 6 | 3/4 |
| 150 | 5 | 2/3 |
| 120 | 4 | 1/2 |
| 75 | 2 ½ | 1/3 |
| 60 | 2 | 1/4 |
| 30 | 1 | 1/8 |
| 15 | ½ | 1 tablespoon |

**WEIGHT**

| G | OZ |
|---|---|
| 15 | 1\2 |
| 30 | 1 |
| 60 | 2 |
| 90 | 3 |
| 110 | 4 |
| 140 | 5 |
| 170 | 6 |
| 200 | 7 |
| 225 | 8 |
| 255 | 9 |

# Under 100 Calories

# Melon & Mint Smoothie

**Serves 1    Calories: 85**

## Ingredients

**200g honeydew melon**

**½ lime**

**2.5cm broccoli stalk**

**150ml coconut water**

**2 to 3 ice cubes**

## Making It

Scoop out the flesh of the melon. Wash the lime skin and slice in half. Wash the broccoli stalk. Add everything to the blender and blend until smooth. Add more water if required.

## Health Benefits

**Honeydew Melon** adds a delicious sweet taste to this smoothie. The antioxidants and vitamin C levels help to boost the immune system and skin health.

**Broccoli** is a great detoxifier as well as a fantastic immunity booster.

**Mint** adds a lovely refreshing taste to this smoothie. Mint is known to have a calming effect on the digestive system.

# Easy Green Smoothie

**Serves 1    Calories: 75**

## Ingredients

**¼ cucumber (approx. 90g)**

**60g spinach**

**1 kiwi (approx. 70g)**

**150ml water**

**2 to 3 ice cubes**

## Making It

Wash and chop the cucumber. Peel and chop the kiwi. Wash the spinach leaves. Add all the ingredients to your blender and blend for 20 to 30 seconds or until smooth. Add more water if you require a thinner consistency.

## Health Benefits

**Cucumbers** are fantastic for hydration – they are 95% water! They contain vitamin K, a vitamin essential for bone health. By also blending the skin of the cucumber you will benefit from the fibre content which helps your digestive tract work more effectively. They are also very low in calories – perfect for weight loss.

**Spinach** is a dark leafy green full to the brim with nutrients. Spinach is low in fat and an excellent source of iron. Spinach is also high in fibre and water. Spinach is also a rich source of potassium, a great energy booster!

**Kiwi** is high in vitamin C and rich in potassium, fibre, folate and vitamins A, K, E and B. They are low in calories yet pack a high nutritional punch.

# Hearty Beets

**Serves 1    Calories: 66**

## Ingredients

**1 small raw beetroot (approx. 80g)**

**60g blueberries (fresh or frozen)**

**1tbsp grated ginger**

**150ml water**

**2 or 3 ice cubes (optional)**

## Making It

Peel and chop the beetroot. Add all the ingredients to your blender and blend until smooth. Add more water if needed.

## Health Benefits

**Beetroot** contains high levels of nitrate which widens the blood vessels, reducing blood pressure and allowing more blood to flow. It cuts the amount of oxygen needed by muscles, making exercise less tiring. Researchers at the University of Exeter discovered that beetroot enables people to exercise for up to 16% longer.

**Tip:** If you can't get used to the earthy beetroot taste, substitute for beetroot juice instead.

# Rocket and Melon

**Serves 1     Calories: 60**

## Ingredients

**30g rocket**

**100g honeydew melon**

**2.5cm fresh root ginger, grated**

**Juice of ½ lemon**

**150ml water**

**2 to 3 ice cubes**

## Making It

Wash the rocket and add to the blender with the water. Blend until smooth. Add the rest of the ingredients and blend. Add more water if needed.

## Health Benefits

**Rocket** (also known as arugula) adds a zesty taste to this smoothie. It is loaded with nutrients including vitamin A, C and zinc. It is also a fantastic source of vitamin K (necessary for bone health). Go for the lighter coloured leaves for a more subtle flavour.

**Ginger** has a distinctive flavour and works well with this smoothie. It is a well-known remedy for reducing feelings of nausea, but it can also help with your immune system and reducing joint inflammation.

**Honeydew Melon** is sweet and juicy. The vitamin A found within it are great for healthy skin. The vitamin C boosts the immune system.

# Almond Green Smoothie

**Serves 1    Calories: 95**

## Ingredients

**4 almonds**

**50g kale**

**50g broccoli**

**150ml almond milk**

**2 to 3 ice cubes**

## Making It

Wash the kale and broccoli. Add all the ingredients to your blender and blend until smooth. Add water if you prefer a thinner smoothie.

## Health Benefits

**Kale** is high in calcium and vitamin C. Kale has many carotenoids, flavonoids and vitamin K.

**Broccoli** is another green vegetable that is high in vitamin C, vitamin K as well as dietary fibre. The levels of carotenoids and flavonoids are higher when consumed raw – so perfect for smoothies.

**Almonds** contain more protein and dietary fibre than many other nuts.

**Almond milk** is rich in antioxidants and 100% plant based. It is naturally low in fat and easy to digest.

# Low Calorie Green Smoothie

**Serves 1    Calories: 96**

## Ingredients

**40g spinach**

**40g Romaine lettuce**

**1 celery stick**

**1 pear**

**Juice of half a lemon**

**150ml water**

**2 to 3 ice cubes**

## Making It

Wash the ingredients. Core and chop the pear. Chop the celery stick. Add the spinach and lettuce with the water to your blender cup and blend until smooth. Add the remaining ingredients and blend. Add more water if you require a thinner consistency.

## Health Benefits

**Spinach** is low in fat, cholesterol but high in zinc, fibre, protein and a range of vitamins. The high iron content makes it a great ingredient to include for those suffering from anaemia.

**Romaine lettuce** is another fantastic source of iron, as well as being high in B vitamins.

**Celery** is very high in vitamin K which is essential for building strong bones and plays a very important role in blood clotting.

**Pears** are incredibly high in fibre, much more so than many other fruits, with most of it contained within the skin – so keep it on when making your smoothie!

# Minty Blackberry

**Serves 1    Calories: 96**

## Ingredients

**200ml skimmed milk**

**80g blackberries**

**6-8 mint leaves**

**2 to 3 ice cubes**

## Making It

Wash the blackberries and mint leaves. Add all the ingredients to your blender and whizz until smooth. Add more water if required.

## Health Benefits

**Blackberries** are high in vitamin C, E and folate. Blackberries are thought to help lower blood pressure. Go for the plumper and blacker looking blackberries for maximum freshness. If they are out of season get some frozen from the supermarket.

**Mint leaves** promote digestion and can help to sooth inflammation in the stomach. They also add a lovely fresh taste to a smoothie!

**Skimmed milk** contains traces of fat and low in calories, it makes a good substitute to full fat milk.

# Grape & Cabbage Smoothie

**Serves 1    Calories: 77**

## Ingredients

**10 red grapes**

**40g savoy green cabbage**

**1 carrot (approx. 60g)**

**Juice of half a lime**

**150ml water**

**2 to 3 ice cubes (optional)**

## Making It

Wash the grapes and cabbage. Wash and chop up the carrot. Add all the ingredients to your blender and blend until smooth. Add more water if required.

## Health Benefits

**Grapes** are high in dietary fibre, vitamin C and vitamin K

**Savoy Green Cabbage** is the sweetest of the cabbages and benefits from being low in calories and high in vitamin C and dietary fibre. Don't consume too much cabbage though, it is known to give you flatulence!

**Carrots** contain the orange coloured beta-carotene which converts into vitamin A, improving your eyesight at night. It's true, carrots can make you see in the dark! Well maybe a little.

# Magical Mint

**Serves 1    Calories: 99**

## Ingredients

**30g baby spinach leaves**

**1 ripe pear**

**4 mint leaves**

**150ml water**

**4 ice cubes**

## Making It

Chop the pear, wash the spinach and mint leaves. Add the water to the blender followed by the leaves, pear, mint and ice cubes. Blend until smooth.

## Health Benefits

**Mint leaves** help to promote digestion as well as healthy weight loss by stimulating the digestive enzymes. Mint can also help to reduce bloating.

**Pears** are very fibrous. About half of the pear's dietary fibre is said to be in the skin. The vitamin C and copper content in a pear make them good for the immune system.

**Spinach** is low in fat, cholesterol and calories yet high in a number of nutrients including iron, vitamins A, C, E and K, magnesium, potassium, manganese and zinc. Wow, what a powerful, nutrient rich green vegetable!

# Cinnamon Strawberries

**Serves 1    Calories: 98**

## Ingredients

**200g strawberries**

**½ tbsp. ground cinnamon**

**Juice of 1 lime**

**1 tbsp. ground flaxseeds (optional)**

**200ml water**

**2 or 3 ice cubes (optional)**

## Making It

Wash and remove the green tops from the strawberries. Add all the ingredients to your blender and blend until smooth.

## Health Benefits

**Strawberries** are very high in vitamin C. In fact, this smoothie contains 149% of your recommended daily allowance of vitamin C!

**Ground flaxseeds** are rich in essential fatty acids – the kind your body can't make. EFA's contribute to the maintenance of normal blood cholesterol levels. Flaxseeds are also rich in protein, iron and magnesium.

**Ground cinnamon** adds a delicious spicy twist to this smoothie. If you can try and use Ceylon cinnamon. Cinnamon is packed with antioxidants and can lower blood sugar levels. For weight loss it can help speed up metabolism and suppress hunger pangs.

# Watermelon Detox

**Serves 1    Calories: 95**

## Ingredients

**200g chopped watermelon**

**60g cucumber**

**3 mint leaves**

**150ml water**

**2 to 3 ice cubes**

## Making It

Chop the watermelon and cucumber up (you can leave the seeds in) and add all the ingredients to your blender cup. Blend on high speed until smooth. Top up with more water if required.

## Health Benefits

This smoothie is great for getting hydrated and detoxing your body. **Watermelon** is made up of 90% water as well as plentiful amounts of antioxidants, amino acids, lycopene and vitamins A, B6 and C.

**Cucumbers** are very low in calories yet high in nutrients, especially vitamins C and K (essential for bone health). Cucumbers are also another great way to stay hydrated healthily as they are over 95% water.

# Strawberry & Pineapple

**Serves 1    Calories: 97**

## Ingredients

**100g fresh or frozen strawberries**

**100g fresh or frozen pineapple chunks**

**1 tbsp. apple cider vinegar**

**150ml water**

**2 to 3 ice cubes (optional)**

## Making It

Add all the ingredients to your blender. If you are using fresh ingredients (rather than frozen) add 2 to 3 ice cubes. Blend until smooth. If you prefer a thinner smoothie, add more water.

## Health Benefits

**Apple cider vinegar** adds a real boost to your smoothie. It is easily available in supermarkets and health food stores. Apple cider vinegar is a versatile ingredient that can be used elsewhere (cooking, cleaning, skincare, in the bath, hair care).

Benefits include assisting in lowering blood sugar levels, helping to make you feel fuller and can help with detoxing by balancing the body's pH levels.

# Strawberry, Mango & Basil Smoothie

**Serves 1    Calories: 99**

## Ingredients

**40g baby spinach**

**6 medium strawberries (fresh or frozen)**

**8 fresh basil leaves**

**80g fresh or frozen mango chunks**

**150ml water**

**2 to 3 ice cubes (optional)**

## Making It

Wash all the ingredients and add to your blender. Blend until smooth. Add more water if required.

## Health Benefits

**Spinach** is a very cleansing green vegetable that is incredibly high in vitamin C, beta-carotene and iron.

**Strawberries** are a fantastic source of vitamin C. The redder the strawberry is the better!

**Basil** is a sweet tasting herb and has a cooling ability which can assist in neutralizing harmful acids in the gut.

**Mango** is high in vitamin C making it a great immune booster. It has high levels of disease fighting carotenoids and is high in magnesium – essential for healthy bones, teeth and muscle contraction.

# Cool Cucumber Smoothie

**Serves 1    Calories: 98**

## Ingredients

**150ml coconut water**

**50g pineapple chunks (fresh or frozen)**

**60g cucumber**

**2 to 3 ice cubes (optional)**

## Making It

Add all the ingredients to your blender. Blend until smooth. If you require a thinner consistency add some water or more coconut water.

## Health Benefits

**Cucumbers** help to reduce water retention. They have a high water content so are great for helping you stay hydrated.

**Pineapple** helps to aid digestion and is a great energy booster. It also helps make a smoothie taste deliciously sweet.

**Coconut water** is naturally low in fat and calories and a great source of potassium. Potassium can help with maintaining normal blood sugar levels and control blood pressure.

# Berry Smoothie

**Serves 1    Calories: 85**

## Ingredients

**80g blackberries (fresh or frozen)**

**80g blueberries (fresh or frozen)**

**80g strawberries (fresh or frozen)**

**150ml water**

**2 to 3 ice cubes (optional)**

## Making It

Add all the ingredients to your blender. Blend until smooth. If you are using completely frozen ingredients you may need to add more water to make the smoothie thinner (unless you prefer it thick!)

## Health Benefits

**Blackberries** are rich in antioxidants, especially vitamin C. They are also low in calories and sodium.

**Blueberries** are a fantastic source of zinc. For such small fruits they boast an incredible array of health benefits including vitamins A and C. They are great for boosting immunity and for eye health.

**Strawberries** are a very rich source of vitamin C as well as an abundant range of minerals including calcium.

# Summer Fruits Smoothie

**Serves 1    Calories: 91**

## Ingredients

**100g mixed berries (fresh or frozen)**

**100ml fresh orange juice**

**50g fat free Greek yoghurt**

**2 to 3 ice cubes (optional)**

## Making It

You can choose your berries – I tend to get a mixed 'Summer Fruits' bag from the supermarket that has blackberries, raspberries, blackcurrants and redcurrants – but you can pick according to what is available. Add all the ingredients to the blender and whizz until smooth. Add water if required.

## Health Benefits

**Mixed berries** have the benefit of being really low in calories yet offering a wide range of rich vitamins and nutrients.  They are particularly high in fibre which is great for weight control.

**Orange juice** is best when it is 100% natural without any added sugars, additives or preservatives. Oranges are most beneficial when eaten whole, however the juice still provides plenty of nutritional value.

**Greek yoghurt** has twice the amount of protein as normal yoghurt. Protein makes you feel fuller for longer making this a great breakfast smoothie.

# Watercress & Pineapple

**Serves 1     Calories: 99**

## Ingredients

**80g pineapple chunks (fresh or frozen)**

**40g watercress**

**150ml water**

**2 to 3 ice cubes (optional)**

## Making It

Wash the watercress and put it in your blender cup, together with the water. Blend until smooth. Add the remaining ingredients and blend. Top up with more water if required.

## Health Benefits

**Watercress** is a nutrient rich leafy green plant, with more vitamin C than oranges. The vitamin A helps with vision health and is packed with vitamin K – necessary for bone strength. It is also a source of iron.

# Red Hot Chilli Strawberries

**Serves 1    Calories: 76**

## Ingredients

**200g strawberries (fresh or frozen)**

**½ red chilli, deseeded**

**40g spinach**

**150ml water**

**2 to 3 ice cubes (optional)**

## Making It

Wash and deseed the red chilli (if you want an extra kick, leave the seeds in!) Wash the other ingredients. Add the water and spinach to the blender and blend until smooth. Add everything else and blend until smooth. Add more water if required.

## Health Benefits

**Strawberries** are not only sweet tasting, they are also nutrient and antioxidant dense.  The calcium content makes them especially good for bone and teeth health.

**Red chilli** is rich in the compound capsaicin. This compound is great for speeding up your metabolism, increasing energy and raising your endorphin levels.

**Spinach** is very high in vitamin C, beta-carotene and iron. Go for the bright green smaller leaves.

# Green Peach Smoothie

**Serves 1    Calories: 71**

## Ingredients

**60g spinach**

**100g sliced peaches**

**150ml almond milk**

**2 to 3 ice cubes**

## Making It

Wash the spinach. Remove the stone from the peach. Add all the ingredients to your blender and whizz until smooth. If you prefer a thinner consistency, top up with either the almond milk or a little water.

**Note:** If you can't get hold of any fresh peaches you can use the canned variety, just make sure you drain away the juice as they contain a lot of sugar.

## Health Benefits

**Peaches** are deliciously sweet, especially when fresh. Peaches are a good for boosting skin health and helping with immunity. The fibre content helps with digestive health.

# Under 200 Calories

# Coconut Strawberry Smoothie

**Serves 1    Calories: 120**

## Ingredients

**80g strawberries**

**150ml coconut milk**

**100g fat free vanilla yoghurt**

**2 to 3 ice cubes**

## Making It

Wash the strawberries. Add all the ingredients to your blender and blend until smooth. Top up with water or more coconut milk if you prefer a thinner smoothie.

## Health Benefits

**Coconut milk** is easy to digest and a great dairy alternative for those with a lactose intolerance. It is a good source of B12 which can assist with reducing tiredness. Naturally low in fat.

# Berries & Cherries

**Serves 1    Calories: 189**

## Ingredients

**50g raspberries**

**50g strawberries**

**50g blueberries**

**50g cherries**

**200ml apple juice**

**2 to 3 ice cubes (optional)**

## Making It

Fresh or frozen fruits work well here. If you are using all frozen you might need to add more liquid to thin it down. Add all the ingredients to the blender and blend until smooth.

## Health Benefits

**Berries** are brilliant for the digestive system owing to their fibre content. Blueberries are particularly high in antioxidants.

# Grapefruit & Mandarin

**Serves 1    Calories: 122**

## Ingredients

**½ pink grapefruit**

**100g mandarins**

**1 medium carrot (approx. 60g)**

**150ml water**

**2 to 3 ice cubes**

## Making It

Peel the grapefruit and remove the seeds. Peel the mandarins. If you can't get any fresh mandarins use the tinned version in juice. Wash and chop the carrot. Add all the ingredients to the blender and blend until smooth. Top up with more water if needed.

## Health Benefits

**Mandarins** are high in vitamin C as well as being an abundant source of fibre.

# Chocco Avocado & Strawberries

**Serves 1    Calories: 186**

## Ingredients

**50g strawberries**

**½ medium avocado (ripe)**

**1tbsp cocoa powder**

**200ml coconut milk**

**2 to 3 ice cubes**

## Making It

Peel the avocado and scoop out the flesh from one half. Add all the ingredients to your blender and blend until smooth. Top up with water if needed.

## Health Benefits

**Avocados** are the ultimate in nutrition. They have more potassium than a banana, high in fibre and loaded with healthy fats.

# Sesame Seeds and Mango

**Serves 1     Calories: 158**

## Ingredients

**1tbsp sesame seeds**

**Juice of ½ lime**

**30g kale**

**100g mango**

**200ml almond milk**

**2 to 3 ice cubes**

## Making It

Wash the kale and put it in your blender cup, together with the almond milk. Blend until smooth. Add the remaining ingredients and blend. Add more almond milk or water if needed.

## Health Benefits

**Sesame Seeds** are a fantastic way of boosting a smoothie. They are full of a rich mix of nutrients including zinc (great for skin elasticity), protein, copper, calcium, iron and large amounts of omega 3 fatty acids.

# Rhubarb & Strawberry Smoothie

**Serves 1    Calories: 106**

## Ingredients

**75g strawberries (fresh or frozen)**

**75g rhubarb (fresh, frozen or tinned in a light syrup)**

**1tbsp honey**

**150ml skimmed milk**

**2 to 3 ice cubes (optional)**

## Making It

If you can't get hold of any fresh or frozen rhubarb and you really want to make this smoothie opt for tinned rhubarb, just try to find one that is in a light syrup or in juice – and don't put the tablespoon of honey in.

If using fresh rhubarb make sure you remove the leaves. Wash and chop the rhubarb. Wash the strawberries and add everything to the blender. Blend until smooth. Top up with water if needed.

## Health Benefits

**Rhubarb** is high in fibre, calcium, antioxidants and vitamin K. It is good for digestive health, bone and muscle health, immunity and health skin and eyes.

# Peach & Passion Smoothie

**Serves 1    Calories: 164**

## Ingredients

**2 passion fruits (approx. 80g)**

**1 fresh peach (approx. 100g) or ½ tin peaches in juice**

**100g 0% fat natural yoghurt**

**200ml coconut water**

**2 to 3 ice cubes (optional)**

## Making It

Cut the passion fruit in half, taking care not to lose any of the juice that might drip out (pour it straight into your blender). Scoop out the flesh, including the seeds. If using a fresh peach, wash the skin and cut in half to remove the stone. Add all the ingredients to your blender and blend until smooth.

## Health Benefits

**Passion fruits** are high in vitamin A, C and potassium. They add a lovely sweet flavour to smoothies – just make sure you get a ripe one. Go for one with a soft, slightly wrinkled skin.  Passion fruit is a very good source of vitamin C.

**Peaches** are great for blending, as long as they are ripe – they should be slightly soft when you squeeze them.  They are very high in beta-carotene which can help with skin and digestive problems.

# Chocolate Almond Smoothie

**Serves 1    Calories: 191**

## Ingredients

**1tsp ground cinnamon**

**1 tbsp. cacao or cocoa powder**

**1 small banana (approx. 100g)**

**1tsp vanilla extract (optional)**

**200ml almond milk**

**2 to 3 ice cubes (optional)**

## Making It

Peel and chop the banana. Add all the ingredients to your blender and blend until smooth. Add some water if you require a thinner consistency.

## Health Benefits

**Almond milk** is a fantastic source of vitamin E, an antioxidant that helps to protect the skin as well as assisting against heart disease. It is easy to digest as well as being naturally low in calories and fat.

**Ground cinnamon** adds a delicious twist to this already tasty smoothie. Cinnamon can help lower blood sugar levels and speed metabolism, making it a great spice to include for weight loss.

**Cacao** is high in magnesium and can help to lower cholesterol and balance blood pressure.

**Bananas** are a great stress buster as well as being rich in the mineral potassium. They can also help lower blood pressure.

**Vanilla extract** is high in many antioxidants which can help protect your body from toxins. The vanilloids present in vanilla can help improve mental performance. The scent of vanilla is often used to reduce food cravings.

# Coconut Banana Smoothie

**Serves 1    Calories: 127**

## Ingredients

**1 small banana (approx. 100g)**

**30g spinach**

**150ml coconut milk**

**2 to 3 ice cubes**

## Making It

Wash the spinach. Peel and chop the banana. Add all the ingredients to your blender and blend until smooth. Add more coconut milk or water if you prefer a thinner smoothie.

# Green Mint Smoothie

## Ingredients

**40g kale**

**1 small green apple (approx. 130g)**

**¼ cucumber (approx. 90g)**

**5 mint leaves**

**150ml water**

**2 to 3 ice cubes (optional)**

## Making It

Wash and chop the cucumber. Wash the kale and mint leaves. Wash, chop and remove the core from the apple. Add the kale, mint and water to your blender and blend until smooth. Add the remaining ingredients and blend until smooth. Add more water if required.

## Health Benefits

**Cucumbers** are very high in water content and low in calories. They are a strong diuretic as well as helping to lower blood pressure.

**Kale** is incredibly high in vitamins A and C. Kale is a very cleansing ingredient, great for cleansing skin from the inside.

**Apples** are great for increasing fibre intake as well as aiding digestion and improving skin health.

**Mint** adds a soothing and refreshing taste to any smoothie. Mint is particularly good for congestion and helping with digestive problems.

# Blueberry & Beetroot

**Serves 1    Calories: 133**

## Ingredients

**30g raw beetroot**

**40g blueberries**

**1 tbsp. grated root ginger**

**½ banana (approx. 60g)**

**150ml coconut water**

**2 to 3 ice cubes (optional)**

## Making It

Peel and chop the beetroot. Wash the blueberries, peel the banana and chop up. Add all the ingredients to your blender and blend until smooth. If required add more water.

## Health Benefits

**Beetroot** can have an earthy taste about it so you might prefer to use beetroot juice instead. Beetroot is a very cleansing vegetable which is fantastic for blood health. Recent research suggests that consuming beetroots can help to boost performance when exercising.

**Blueberries** are a good source of fibre, vitamin K and C, making them fantastic for boosting your immunity.

**Ginger** adds a sharp zing to this smoothie, providing you with a boost of energy.

**Bananas** are a great fruit to blend up in a smoothie. Although higher in calories they are full of fibre, minerals, vitamins and carbohydrates – great for keeping you feeling full and full of energy.

**Coconut water** is also a fantastic source of potassium. Potassium helps to maintain normal blood pressure and works to beat tiredness. Coconut water is also low in calories and fat free.

# Berry Breakfast Smoothie

**Serves 1    Calories: 139**

## Ingredients

**60g blueberries**

**60g raspberries**

**½ banana (about 60g)**

**200ml almond milk**

**2 to 3 ice cubes (optional)**

## Making It

Wash the blueberries and raspberries. Peel and chop the banana. Add all the ingredients to your blender and blend until smooth. Add some water if required.

## Health Benefits

**Blueberries** are a tasty fruit to add to any smoothie. They are full of antioxidant nutrients such as vitamins A and C, as well as bioflavonoids.

**Raspberries** are another very rich source of antioxidants; the phytonutrients in raspberries can help improve learning capacity – great brain power!

**Bananas** are great for making you feel fuller for longer as well as for distressing and lowering high blood pressure.

**Almond milk** makes a great dairy alternative and is low in calories and fat, yet high in vitamin E.

# Apple & Spinach Smoothie

**Serves 1    Calories: 102**

## Ingredients

**60g spinach**

**1 green apple (approx. 140g)**

**¼ lemon (unwaxed)**

**200ml water**

**2 to 3 ice cubes (optional)**

## Making It

Wash the spinach and lemon. Wash, chop and remove the core from the apple. Add all the water and spinach to your blender and blend until smooth. Add the remaining ingredients and blend. Add more water if you require a thinner consistency.

## Health Benefits

**Spinach** is incredibly rich in vitamin C, beta-carotene and iron.

**Golden delicious** apples contain no fat, are high in fibre and an excellent source of vitamin C.

**Lemons** are rich in vitamin C and contain a high amount of minerals and potassium.

# Minty Beetroot Smoothie

**Serves 1    Calories: 138**

## Ingredients

**30g raw beetroot**

**5 mint leaves**

**1 small banana (approx. 100g)**

**1tbsp grated root ginger**

**200ml almond milk**

**2 to 3 ice cubes (optional)**

## Making It

Wash, peel and chop the raw beetroot. Wash the mint. Peel and chop the banana. Add all the ingredients to your blender and blend until smooth. Add some water if required.

## Health Benefits

**Beetroot** does have a soil like taste to it, especially when blended. If you find the taste too much, use beetroot juice instead (either shop bought or in your own juicer). Beetroot is a very cleansing root vegetable, rich in immune boosting beta carotene and folate.

**Mint** is a refreshing and aromatic herb. Mint is particularly good for improving digestion and can help reduce nausea. The menthol in mint can also be good for congestion.

**Bananas** are a fantastic energy booster and taste great with mint and ginger. They are high in potassium.

**Ginger** is another ingredient that helps with digestion and reduce nausea. It can also help with cold symptoms such as sore throats and congestion.

**Almond milk** is low in calories and fat, a fantastic dairy alternative.

# Blueberry & Spinach

**Serves 1    Calories: 133**

## Ingredients

**200g blueberries (fresh or frozen)**

**40g spinach**

**200ml coconut water**

**Ice cubes (optional)**

## Making It

Wash the blueberries and spinach. Add the spinach and coconut water to your blender and blend until smooth. Add the remaining ingredients and blend. Add water if you require a thinner smoothie.

## Health Benefits

**Blueberries** are rich in vitamin C, vitamin K and manganese. Vitamin K and manganese are both vital for bone health.

**Coconut water** provides natural hydration for the body as well as being a great source of potassium.

**Spinach** is a great energy booster owing to its high iron content. It is great for improving immunity owing to high levels of vitamin C.

# Spring Greens & Berries

**Serves 1    Calories: 147**

## Ingredients

**60g spring greens**

**200ml coconut water**

**60g blueberries**

**60g raspberries**

**2 to 3 ice cubes**

## Making It

Wash the spring greens, blueberries and raspberries. Add the greens and coconut water to your blender and blend until smooth. Add the remaining ingredients to your blender. Add water if you require a thinner smoothie.

## Health Benefits

**Spring greens** make a great alternative to spinach and kale. They are high in vitamin C and vitamin K. Vitamin K is good for building bone strength.

# Cantaloupe & Raspberry

**Serves 1    Calories: 189**

## Ingredients

**150g cantaloupe melon**

**100g raspberries**

**100g fat free vanilla yoghurt**

**2 to 3 ice cubes**

## Making It

Chop the cantaloupe melon into small chunks. Add all the ingredients to your blender and blend until smooth. Top up with water if you require a thinner consistency.

## Health Benefits

**Cantaloupe melon** provides vitamin C as well as beta and alpha-carotene which convert into Vitamin A in the body. As with other melons they are also very high in water yet low in calories. Great for rehydrating without bumping up the calorie intake.

# Carrot, Ginger & Lemon Smoothie

**Serves 1    Calories: 108**

## Ingredients

**1 large carrot (approx. 70g)**

**½ lemon (unwaxed)**

**1 inch fresh root ginger, grated**

**150ml fresh orange juice**

**2 to 3 ice cubes**

## Making It

Wash the carrots and lemon. Chop the carrot up. Slice the lemon. Add all the ingredients to your blender and blend until smooth. Add water if you require a thinner smoothie.

## Health Benefits

**Carrots** add a lovely sweet taste to this smoothie. Carrots are packed with vitamins and minerals. Carrots are well known for their high beta-carotene content, an antioxidant responsible for healthy skin and vision.

# Papaya & Parsley Smoothie

**Serves 1    Calories: 119**

## Ingredients

**200g papaya**

**1 lime**

**20g parsley**

**150ml water**

**2 to 3 ice cubes**

## Making It

Make sure you pick a ripe papaya (it should have a slight orange hint to it). Prepare the papaya by cutting it in half length ways and scooping out the black seeds. Cut out the flesh with a small sharp knife. Wash the skin of the lime and slice. Wash the parsley. Add all the ingredients to the blender and whizz until smooth. Add more water if required.

## Health Benefits

**Papaya** is a tropical powerhouse packed full with beta-carotene, fibre, vitamin C and enzymes that aid digestion.

**Limes** add to the tasty tropical blend of this smoothie. They also help with digestion, eye health and skin care.

**Parsley** is a super health herb to add to any dish and works surprisingly well in a smoothie. Parsley is super high in chlorophyll, making it fantastic for cleansing the body. It is also well known for helping with digestion as well as being full of minerals and vitamins.

# Avocado & Orange Smoothie

**Serves 1    Calories: 193**

## Ingredients

**60g spring greens**

**½ ripe avocado (fresh or frozen)**

**150ml fresh orange juice**

**2 to 3 ice cubes (optional)**

## Making It

Wash the spring greens. If using a fresh avocado, slice it in half and scoop out the flesh from one side. Add all the ingredients to your blender and blend until smooth. Add some water if you require a thinner consistency.

## Health Benefits

**Avocado** contains oleic acid, a monounsaturated fat that is great for a healthy heart. The beauty of including avocado in your smoothies is that they contain all the essential amino acids your body requires. The fat content helps to satisfy the appetite which in turn will assist with weight management.

**Fresh orange juice** contains lots of vitamins but of course has none of the fibre content.

# Prune and Vanilla Smoothie

**Serves 1    Calories: 132**

## Ingredients

**3 prunes**

**1tsp ground cinnamon**

**200ml vanilla soya milk**

**2 to 3 ice cubes**

## Making It

Add all the ingredients to your blender and blend until smooth. Add some water if required.

## Health Benefits

**Prunes** are not only great for keeping bowel movements regular, they also act as an appetite suppressant. They do this by slowing down how quickly the food leaves the stomach, making you feel fuller for longer.

**Cinnamon** is great for helping with stomach upsets as well as lowering blood sugar levels.

**Vanilla soya milk** is 100% plant based and naturally low in saturated fat. It is a great source of calcium and contains vitamins B2, B12 and D.

# Goji and Strawberry Smoothie

## Ingredients

**25g dried goji berries**

**200ml coconut water**

**100g strawberries**

**2 to 3 ice cubes**

## Making It

Add all the ingredients to your blender and whizz until smooth. Add some water if you require a thinner consistency.

## Health Benefits

**Goji berries** can help boost the immune system as well as help support healthy skin owing the high beta-carotene content.

**Strawberries** not only taste good, they are also packed with folate which is important for brain function. Strawberries are also rich in vitamin C. Make sure you go for strawberries that are completely red.

# Romaine & Pear Smoothie

**Serves 1    Calories: 115**

## Ingredients

**6 Romaine lettuce leaves**

**30g spinach**

**1 ripe pear (approx. 130g)**

**Juice of 1 lime**

**150ml water**

**2 to 3 ice cubes**

## Making It

Chop up and remove the core from the pear. Wash the spinach and romaine leaves. Slice the lime in half and juice both halves. Add the lettuce, spinach and water to your blender and blend until smooth. Add the remaining ingredients to your blender and blend. Add more water if required.

## Health Benefits

**Romaine lettuce** is rich in the B vitamins as well as manganese, potassium and iron.

**Spinach** is high in vitamin K, an essential nutrient for bone health. The high levels of vitamin A helps boost immunity, eye health as well as skin health.

**Pears** are low in calories yet high in vitamin C, dietary fibre, potassium and carbohydrates. They are perfect for aiding constipation as well as keeping your digestive system healthy.

**Lime juice** has a wide range of healthy attributes, one of which is the citric acid content which is an excellent fat burner.

# Cherry & Peach Smoothie

**Serves 1    Calories: 140**

## Ingredients

**150g peach slices**

**60g cherries (pitted) fresh or frozen**

**200ml almond milk**

**Juice of 1 lime**

**2 to 3 ice cubes (optional)**

## Making It

If you can't get fresh peaches to slice you can use the tinned variety, just make sure you get peaches in juice rather than syrup.

Add all the ingredients to your blender and whizz until smooth. Add some water if you prefer a thinner consistency.

## Health Benefits

**Cherries** are rich in flavonoids including anthocyanins which are thought to have anti-inflammatory properties.

# Raspberry & Cinnamon

**Serves 1    Calories: 182**

## Ingredients

**200g raspberries**

**1 tsp ground cinnamon**

**200ml soya milk**

**2 to 3 ice cubes (optional)**

## Making It

Wash the raspberries. Add all the ingredients to your blender. Blend until smooth. Add additional water if required.

## Health Benefits

**Raspberries** are high in antioxidants. They are a good source of fibre, vitamin K, fibre and omega fatty acids. Raspberries are recommended for digestive health, healthy skin and for boosting the immune system.

**Cinnamon** not only adds a deliciously warm flavour to this smoothie, it also has very high antioxidant levels. Cinnamon is used in many cultures to help fight infections and illnesses.

**Soya Milk** is a good dairy free milk alternative. It contains no cholesterol and is high in calcium.

# Coconut Mango Smoothie

**Serves: 1   Calories: 155**

## Ingredients

**60g chopped mango (fresh or frozen)**

**1 small ripe banana (approx. 100g)**

**150ml coconut water**

**2 to 3 ice cubes (optional)**

## Making It

Peel and chop the banana. Add all the ingredients to your blender and blend until smooth. Add more water if necessary.

## Health Benefits

**Mangoes** provide high levels of antioxidants including vitamins A, C and E – fantastic for immune strength, skin and eye health.

**Bananas** provide energy and are great for making you feel fuller for longer.

# Banana and Greens

**Serves 1    Calories: 134**

## Ingredients

**30g kale**

**30g spinach**

**1 small ripe banana (approx. 100g)**

**150ml water**

**2 to 3 ice cubes (optional)**

## Making It

Wash the kale and spinach. Peel the banana and chop up (if using fresh). Add the kale, spinach and water to the blender and blend until smooth. Add the remaining ingredients to your blender and whizz until smooth. Add more water if required.

# Apricot Smoothie

**Serves 1     Calories: 181**

## Ingredients

**30g (about 5) dried apricots**

**40g spinach**

**100g carrots**

**½ unwaxed lemon**

**250ml coconut water**

**2 to 3 ice cubes (optional)**

## Making It

Wash the spinach, carrots and lemon. Chop the carrots up. Add the spinach and water to your blender and blend until smooth. Add the remaining ingredients to your blender and whizz until smooth. Depending on the power of your blender you might need to blend for a longer time to ensure the apricots become smooth.

## Health Benefits

**Dried apricots** have less vitamin C than the fresh variety but they contain more fibre, protein, carotenoids and iron. Iron is particularly good for increasing energy levels especially for those suffering from anaemia.

# Marvellous Mango

**Serves 1    Calories: 182**

## Ingredients

**100g fresh or frozen chopped ripe mango**

**100g fat free vanilla yoghurt**

**150ml skimmed milk**

**Juice of 1 lime**

**2 to 3 ice cubes (optional)**

## Making It

Pour the milk and yoghurt in your blender. Add the chopped mango and lime juice. Add ice cubes if you are not using frozen mango. Blend for about 20 to 30 seconds or until smooth.

## Health Benefits

**Mangoes** are a great source of fibre making them great for weight loss. They are also rich in vitamin A and flavonoids, including beta-carotene making them beneficial for healthy vision.

**Greek yoghurt** is really high in protein which can assist in any weight loss program by making you feel fuller for longer.

**Skimmed milk** is low in fat and calories yet still high in calcium. Calcium is essential for strong bones and teeth. Calcium also reduces the risk of osteoporosis which is a higher risk for women as they age.

# Watermelon & Strawberry

**Serves 1    Calories: 125**

## Ingredients

**150g watermelon**

**60g fresh or frozen strawberries**

**100g fat free Greek yoghurt**

**2 to 3 ice cubes (optional)**

**Water (optional)**

## Making It

Add all the ingredients to your blender. Blend for 20 to 30 seconds or until smooth.  If the smoothie is too thick for you, add a small amount of water and blend again. Repeat until the smoothie is at your preferred consistency.

## Health Benefits

**Watermelon** has high water content, keeping you well hydrated. Watermelon contains vitamins A and C and potassium. If you are blending the seeds they are a good source of protein and magnesium.

# Cider Grapes

**Serves 1    Calories: 195**

## Ingredients

**30 seedless red grapes**

**2tbsp apple cider vinegar**

**1tbsp honey**

**150ml coconut water**

**2 to 3 ice cubes**

## Making It

Add all the ingredients to your blender. Blend for 20 to 30 seconds or until smooth. Depending on the power of your blender you might still have some of the skin of the grapes in your smoothie.

## Health Benefits

**Red Grapes** not only make a great snack, they also work well in a smoothie. They are richer in antioxidants than the green variety. They are high in dietary fibre, vitamins C and K.

**Apple cider vinegar** has been shown to increase feelings of fullness and increase metabolism.

# Minty Avocado

**Serves 1    Calories: 140**

## Ingredients

**½ ripe avocado (fresh or frozen)**

**½ lime (plus a hint of lime zest)**

**5 fresh mint leaves**

**200ml of coconut water**

**2 to 3 ice cubes**

## Making It

Wash the mint leaves. Grate a small amount of the zest off the lime to use and then peel the lime and use ½ of it in the blender. Add all the other ingredients including the lime zest to your blender. If you are not using frozen avocado then you can add some ice cubes as well. Blend for 20 to 30 seconds or until smooth. Add more water if needed.

## Health Benefits

**Avocados** are considered a superfood owing to their abundance of nutrients. They are high in so many healthy attributes, including their support of the immune system. They contain loads of fibre, potassium, healthy omega-3 fatty acids and vitamins A, C and E. They are also a fantastic source of fibre.

# Honeydew Melon & Apple

**Serves 1    Calories: 122**

## Ingredients

**100g honeydew melon**

**1 kiwi (approx. 80g)**

**½ green apple (approx. 60g)**

**1 tbsp. lemon juice (approx. 15ml)**

**150ml water**

**Ice cubes (optional)**

## Making It

Slice up the honeydew melon and scoop out the flesh. Peel and chop the kiwi. Wash and chop the apple, removing the core. Add all the ingredients to your blender and blend until smooth. Add more water if required.

## Health Benefits

**Honeydew Melon** adds a delicious sweet taste to this smoothie. The antioxidants and vitamin C levels help to boost the immune system and skin health.

**Kiwis** are high in vitamins C, A and E, potassium and lutein, making them great for strengthening the immune system and eye health. They are also a good source of carbohydrates.

**Apples** are a fantastic source of flavonoids as well as pectin, a soluble fibre that helps to slow the absorption of cholesterol and sugar into the bloodstream.

# Strawberry & Lime

**Serves 1    Calories: 176**

## Ingredients

**200g of strawberries, fresh or frozen**

**Juice of 1 lime**

**1 tbsp. Chia seeds**

**150ml of water**

**2 to 3 ice cubes (optional)**

## Making It

Wash the strawberries and add all the ingredients to your blender and blend until smooth. If you require a thinner consistency please add some water or more coconut water.

## Health Benefits

**Chia Seeds** are packed high with omega-3s as well as being a fantastic source of protein and fibre. Chia seeds bulk out when they are mixed with liquid, they help to decrease hunger whilst boosting metabolism.

# Almond Breakfast Smoothie

**Serves 1    Calories: 149**

## Ingredients

**50g blueberries (fresh or frozen)**

**1tbsp maple syrup (or honey)**

**10g (about 10) raw almonds**

**150ml unsweetened almond milk**

**2 to 3 ice cubes (optional)**

## Making It

Add all the ingredients to your blender. If you are not using frozen blueberries you may want to add the ice cubes. Blend for 20 to 30 seconds or until smooth. If you are not using a high speed blender your smoothie might have a few unblended almonds in it. Add water or more almond milk if you require a thinner consistency.

## Health Benefits

**Almonds** are a fantastic source of vitamin E. Vitamin E is a great antioxidant that is necessary to keep a healthy blood supply and heart. Vitamin E can also help reduce the symptoms of the menopause.

**Blueberries** are a rich source of antioxidants and vitamin C. They are thought to be good for strengthening the immune system and reducing the risk of a heart attack. They are also low in calories.

**Maple Syrup** is a great natural sweetener to add to your smoothie. It is loaded with essential nutrients such as zinc and manganese. Manganese helps improve bone strength and is important for healthy brain function. Maple syrup is also rich in vitamins such as vitamin A and the B vitamins. Try and use completely natural maple syrup with no added extras.

# Low Cal Fruit Smoothie

**Serves 1    Calories: 150**

## Ingredients

**40g spinach**

**1 kiwi**

**100g peach slices**

**6 strawberries (fresh or frozen)**

**150ml water**

**2 to 3 ice cubes (optional)**

## Making It

Wash the spinach, strawberries, peel the kiwi and slice up. You can either use a fresh peach or take them from a tin. If you are using tinned peaches opt for slices in juice rather than syrup.

Add all the ingredients to your blender and blend until smooth. If you prefer a thinner consistency add more water.

# Raspberry & Chia Smoothie

**Serves 1    Calories: 167**

## Ingredients

**100g raspberries (fresh or frozen)**

**2tbsp chia seeds**

**100g fat free Greek yoghurt**

**150ml unsweetened almond milk**

**2 to 3 ice cubes (optional)**

## Making It

Add all the ingredients to your blender and whizz for 20 to 30 seconds or until smooth. Add some water if you prefer a thinner consistency.

## Health Benefits

**Chia Seeds** are packed high with omega-3s as well as being a fantastic source of protein and fibre. Chia seeds bulk out when they are mixed with liquid, they help to decrease hunger whilst boosting metabolism.

**Raspberries** are low in fat and calories yet high in dietary fibre and antioxidants.

# Blueberry & Avocado Smoothie

**Serves 1    Calories: 156**

## Ingredients

**60g spinach**

**1tbsp fresh root ginger, grated**

**100g blueberries**

**½ ripe avocado**

**150ml water**

**2 to 3 ice cubes (optional)**

## Making It

Wash the spinach and blueberries. Slice the avocado in half and scoop out the flesh. Add the spinach and water to your blender and blend until smooth. Add the remaining ingredients and blend. Add more water if required.

## Health Benefits

**Blueberries** may be small in size but they are a powerhouse of antioxidants. They are known for a wide range of health benefits including eye and skin health, digestive health, boosted immunity and brain function. They are great in smoothies but they also make a fantastic snack on.

# Fig & Banana Smoothie

**Serves 1    Calories: 171**

## Ingredients

**3 fresh figs**

**1 small banana (approx. 100g)**

**150ml coconut water**

**2 to 3 ice cubes**

## Making It

Wash the figs. As you can eat the whole fig (skin included) just chop them up and put them in your blender. Peel and chop the banana and add to the blender with the coconut water and ice cubes. Blend until smooth. Top up with more coconut water or plain water if required.

## Health Benefits

**Figs** are good for the digestive system owing to their high fibre content. The vitamin K and magnesium help to maintain health bones.

# Green Kiwi Smoothie

**Serves 1    Calories: 140**

## Ingredients

**1 kiwi**

**1 tbsp. grated ginger**

**40g spinach**

**40g cucumber**

**1 celery stalk (approx. 30g)**

**150ml coconut water**

**2 to 3 ice cubes (optional)**

## Making It

Peel and chop the kiwi. Wash the spinach, celery and cucumber. Chop the cucumber and celery up into smaller pieces. Add all the ingredients to your blender and blend until smooth. Add some water if you prefer a thinner smoothie.

## Health Benefits

**Kiwi** is packed with vitamin C. In fact, just 1 kiwi will provide you with 100% of your daily vitamin C requirements. Vitamin C is a great antioxidant which helps to fight infections.

**Celery** is great for lowering cholesterol, an immune booster as well as assisting with eye health.

# Ginger and Pear Smoothie

**Serves 1    Calories: 136**

## Ingredients

**1 pear**

**1tbsp fresh root ginger, grated**

**Juice of ½ lime**

**100ml water**

**2 to 3 ice cubes (optional)**

## Making It

Wash and core the pear. Add all the ingredients to your blender and blend until smooth. Add more water if required.

## Health Benefits

**Pears** are very high in fibre which is great for bowel health and reducing bad cholesterol. Keep the skin on though as this is where most of the fibre is located.

# Under 300 Calories

# Smooth Blackberries

**Serves 1    Calories: 238**

## Ingredients

**1 medium ripe banana**

**150g blackberries**

**40g spinach**

**200ml water**

**2 to 3 ice cubes**

## Making It

Wash the ingredients as required. Add the spinach and water to your blender and blend until smooth. Add the remaining ingredients and blend until smooth. Add more water if required.

## Health Benefits

**Bananas** are great for heart health and digestion. They contain good amounts of fibre and other nutrients that can be good for eye health.

**Blackberries** are rich in antioxidants especially vitamin C, making them great for a strong immune system.

# Berry Tasty Smoothie

**Serves 1     Calories: 209**

## Ingredients

**80g strawberries**

**60g raspberries**

**50g dried cranberries**

**150ml water**

**2 to 3 ice cubes (optional)**

## Making It

Wash the strawberries and raspberries. Add all the ingredients to the blender and blend until smooth. Add more water if required.

## Health Benefits

**Dried Cranberries** have some of the highest antioxidants properties of any other fruit. They are high in vitamin C and manganese.

# Breakfast Muesli Smoothie

**Serves 1    Calories: 297**

## Ingredients

**30g muesli**

**1tbsp peanut butter**

**60g raspberries**

**150ml soya milk**

**2 or 3 ice cubes (optional)**

## Making It

Wash the raspberries. Add all the ingredients to your blender and blend until smooth. Add some water if required.

## Health Benefits

**Muesli** is a great addition, helping you feel fuller for longer, making it a great breakfast smoothie. It is high in whole grains and fibre. If you are buying supermarket muesli (as opposed to making your own), make sure it has no added sugar.

**Peanut butter** is at its best when there are only nuts in the ingredients. You can buy 'only peanuts' peanut butter, or if you own a high speed blender you can make your own, it will last a couple of months if kept in the fridge. Peanut butter does have to be eaten in moderation as part of a weight loss diet but it is high in protein, Vitamin E, magnesium, potassium and vitamin B6.

**Soya Milk** is a good source of protein and the B vitamins. It is low in sugars and saturated fat and makes a great dairy alternative.

**Raspberries** not only taste great, they are also a great source of vitamin C, fibre, manganese and vitamin K.

# Apple & Pecan Smoothie

**Serves 1    Calories: 251**

## Ingredients

**1 small green apple (approx. 140g)**

**5 pecans**

**60g pineapple chunks (fresh or frozen)**

**150ml coconut water**

**2 to 3 ice cubes (optional)**

## Making It

Wash, chop and remove the core from the apple. Add all the ingredients to your blender and blend until smooth. Top up with water or more coconut water if required.

## Health Benefits

**Pecans** are a great source of energy and although high in calories, they pack so many antioxidants its worth including them in a smoothie from time to time. They are rich in omega-6 fatty acids.

# Plum & Banana Smoothie

**Serves 1    Calories: 207**

## Ingredients

**2 plums (approx. 65g each)**

**50g blueberries**

**1 small ripe banana (approx. 80g)**

**150ml water**

**2 to 3 ice cubes (optional)**

## Making It

Wash and pit the plums. Wash the blueberries. Peel and chop the banana. Add all the ingredients to your blender and blend until smooth. Add more water if needed.

## Health Benefits

**Plums** are juicy and sweet as well as being rich in antioxidants. They are low in calories and high in fibre, perfect for weight loss and maintenance!

# Broccoli Green Smoothie

**Serves 1    Calories: 297**

## Ingredients

**1 small pear (approx. 150g)**

**80g frozen broccoli**

**150ml fresh apple juice**

**½ ripe avocado (approx. 60g)**

**2 to 3 ice cubes (optional)**

## Making It

Chop the pear up and remove the core and seeds. Cut the avocado in half and scoop out the flesh from one half. Add all the ingredients to your blender and blend until smooth. Top up with a little water if required.

## Health Benefits

**Broccoli** is very high in vitamin C as well as being a great source of dietary fibre. Broccoli is a great immunity booster.

# Hazelnut & Avocado Smoothie

**Serves 1    Calories: 252**

## Ingredients

**20g roasted chopped hazelnuts**

**½ ripe avocado**

**200ml hazelnut milk**

**2 to 3 ice cubes (optional)**

## Making It

Slice the avocado in half and scoop out the flesh. Add all the ingredients to your blender and blend until smooth. Add some water if required.

## Health Benefits

**Roasted hazelnuts** are high in fibre, protein and monounsaturated fats. They are rich in antioxidants such as vitamin E and flavonoids.

**Hazelnut milk** is 100% plant based and is a source of vitamin B12, necessary for healthy nervous system. It is low in saturated fat.

# Coconut and Mango Smoothie

**Serves 1     Calories: 230**

## Ingredients

**50g coconut flesh**

**30g spinach**

**60g chopped mango**

**Juice of ½ a lime**

**150ml water**

**2 to 3 ice cubes (optional)**

## Making It

You can buy a whole coconut and take the flesh out – or buy a 'snack pack' of coconut chunks that supermarkets tend to sell. I find the coconut chunks more time efficient and there is less wastage.

Wash the spinach and add to the blender with the water. Blend until smooth. Add the remaining ingredients and blend. Top up with more water if needed.

## Health Benefits

**Coconuts** is high in fat but it is high quality fat. Coconut is high in fibre, manganese, vitamin C and copper. It is good for increased energy, strong bones, digestive health and joint health.

# Strawberry, Pumpkin & Almond

**Serves 1    Calories: 225**

## Ingredients

**100g strawberries**

**25g pumpkin seeds**

**200ml almond milk**

**2 to 3 ice cubes (optional)**

## Making It

Wash the strawberries. Add all the ingredients to your blender and blend until smooth. Add additional water if required.

## Health Benefits

**Almond milk** is low in calories and fat. It is a good source of calcium and vitamins B2, B12, D and E.

**Pumpkin seeds** are great for heart health due to the high levels of polyunsaturated fats. These tasty seeds also contain high levels of protein, zinc and various forms of vitamin E.

# Avocado Boost Smoothie

**Serves 1    Calories: 242**

## Ingredients

**½ ripe avocado**

**½ lemon (unwaxed)**

**1 tbsp. grated root ginger**

**150ml fresh apple juice**

**1tbsp ground flaxseed**

**2 to 3 ice cubes (optional)**

## Making It

Cut the avocado in half and scoop out the flesh of one side. Wash the lemon and cut in half. Add all the ingredients to your blender and blend until smooth. Add some water if you prefer a thinner smoothie.

## Health Benefits

**Avocados** are high in healthy fats and a good source of dietary fibre. The nutrients and fatty acids are great for maintaining healthy skin.

**Lemons** contain a lot of vitamin C with much of it found in the skin. Try to go for unwaxed lemons so you can simply wash them and blend.

**Ginger** has a very high level of antioxidants. It is well known for its traditional uses of reducing nausea.

**Flaxseeds** add a super nutritious boost to smoothies. They are high in fibre, omeg-3s and antioxidants.

# Pistachio Smoothie

**Serves 1    Calories: 217**

## Ingredients

**20 shelled pistachios (approx. 15g)**

**60g strawberries**

**1 kiwi**

**100g 0% fat Greek yoghurt**

**150ml almond milk**

**2 to 3 ice cubes (optional)**

## Making It

Add all the ingredients to your blender and blend until smooth. Top up with more almond milk or water if needed.

## Health Benefits

**Pistachio nuts** are a fantastic source of monounsaturated fats as well as being rich in manganese, copper and vitamin B6.

# Green Pear Smoothie

**Serves 1    Calories: 263**

## Ingredients

**1 small pear (150g)**

**30g spinach**

**3 sprigs of parsley**

**¼ cucumber (75g)**

**½ avocado (80g)**

**½ tsp spirulina (optional)**

**150ml water**

**2 to 3 ice cubes**

## Making It

Chop and core the pear, leaving the skin on. Scoop the flesh out of half the avocado. Wash the remaining ingredients. Add everything to your blender and blend until smooth. Add more water if required.

## Health Benefits

**Parsley** is a rich source of vitamins A, C and K. Vitamin K is great for bone health. Parsley is also high in iron content so brilliant for energy levels.

**Pears** are great energy boosters owing to the high content of carbohydrates and potassium. The high fibre content is good for the digestive system.

# Cashew, Mango & Lime

**Serves 1    Calories: 234**

## Ingredients

**25g cashew nuts**

**100g mango chunks**

**1 lime**

**150ml water**

**2 to 3 ice cubes (optional)**

## Making It

Slice and scoop out the mango flesh (unless using frozen). Wash the lime and slice. Add all the ingredients to your blender and blend until smooth. Add more water if required.

## Health Benefits

**Cashew nuts** are high in fibre, minerals, protein (a small handful has almost the same amount as an egg), as well as monounsaturated fatty acid.

**Mangos** are rich in vitamins A, C and E. They are great for healthy skin and eyes.

**Limes** are an excellent source of vitamin C as well as being rich in antioxidants.

# Banana & Blackberries

**Serves 1    Calories: 245**

## Ingredients

**1 small ripe banana**

**150g blackberries**

**40g spinach**

**40g mixed greens**

**150ml water**

**2 to 3 ice cubes (optional)**

## Making It

Wash the ingredients as required. Add the spinach, mixed greens and water to your blender and blend. Add remaining ingredients and blend until smooth. Add more water if required.

## Health Benefits

**Blackberries** feel like a real treat in any smoothie. They are good for digestive health as well as being a great immunity booster.

# Cashew & Carrot Smoothie

**Serves 1    Calories: 277**

## Ingredients

**2 (approx. 120g) medium carrots**

**100g fat free Greek yoghurt**

**25g cashew nuts**

**200ml almond milk**

**2 to 3 ice cubes**

## Making It

Wash the carrots and chop up. Add everything to your blender and blend until smooth. Add some water if required.

## Health Benefits

**Carrots** are one of the richest sources of beta-carotene, which your body then turns into vitamin A. They also have no fat or cholesterol. Perfect for weight loss!

**Cashew nuts** are a sweet addition to this smoothie. They are full of antioxidants, energy, vitamins and minerals. They are also low in cholesterol and sodium.

# Spring Green Smoothie

**Serves 1    Calories: 259**

## Ingredients

**60g sliced spring greens**

**1 small ripe banana (fresh or frozen)**

**60g fresh or frozen strawberries**

**1tbsp ground flaxseeds**

**150ml water**

**2 to 3 ice cubes**

## Making It

Wash ingredients and add the spring greens and water to your blender. Blend until smooth. Add the remaining ingredients to your blender. Add more water if you require a thinner consistency.

## Health Benefits

**Ground flaxseeds** make a fantastic boost to a smoothie. They are a good source of magnesium, fibre, iron, zinc and a brilliant natural source of omega 3.

# Banana, Oat & Chia Smoothie

**Serves 1    Calories: 290**

## Ingredients

**1 small ripe banana**

**1tbsp chia seeds**

**150ml oat milk**

**2 to 3 ice cubes (optional)**

## Making It

Add all the ingredients to your blender and blend until smooth. Add water if a thinner consistency is required.

## Health Benefits

**Oat milk** is low in fat, high in fibre with no added sugars. It is easy to digest. It has a natural taste with added calcium and vitamins B2, B12 and D.

# Orange & Cranberries

**Serves 1    Calories: 213**

## Ingredients

**100g fresh, frozen or dried cranberries**

**100g low fat vanilla yoghurt**

**150ml fresh orange juice**

**2 to 3 ice cubes (optional)**

## Making It

Add all the ingredients to your blender and whizz until smooth. Add some water if you prefer a thinner consistency.

## Health Benefits

**Fresh cranberries** will be available in some supermarkets depending on the season. Some stores sell frozen cranberries. If you can't get either go for dried cranberries. Dried cranberries do have more sugar and less vitamin C than fresh. Cranberries are good for healthy skin, immunity health, and digestive health and are a well-known remedy for urine infections.

# Kiwi & Avocado Smoothie

**Serves 1    Calories: 224**

## Ingredients

**40g kale**

**1 kiwi (approx. 80g)**

**½ avocado (fresh or frozen)**

**1tbsp honey**

**150ml almond milk**

**2 to 3 ice cubes (optional)**

## Making It

Peel the kiwi and slice up. If using fresh avocado cut it in half and scoop out the flesh of one half. Wash the kale and add it to the blender with the almond milk. Blend until smooth. Add all the remaining ingredients to your blender and whizz until smooth.

# Seedy Green Smoothie

**Serves 1    Calories: 245**

## Ingredients

**60g spinach**

**½ medium ripe banana**

**1tbsp mixed seeds**

**150ml soya milk**

**2 to 3 ice cubes (optional)**

## Making It

Place all the ingredients in your blender and whizz for 20 to 30 seconds or until smooth. Add more water if required.

## Health Benefits

You can either make your own **mixed seeds** combination or buy a pack from the supermarket. Choose from sunflower, sesame, pumpkin, hemp, flax and chia. Any mix of these will provide you with high levels of antioxidants and health benefits.

# Frozen Pineapple & Coconut

**Serves 1    Calories: 216**

## Ingredients

**100g frozen Pineapple**

**50g frozen banana (chopped)**

**60ml coconut milk**

## Making It

This makes for a delightful dessert and is actually quite filling.

Put the pineapple and banana in your blender. Try and add as much of the cream as you can from the coconut milk (you can try standing it upside down to separate it before opening it). Switch your blender on and blend until smooth. You can eat it straight away or pop it in a freezer safe container for 1 hour until firmer.

## Health Benefits

**Coconut milk** is rich in fibre and full of minerals and vitamins. It is completely dairy free so handy for those who are lactose intolerant. Coconut milk is high in iron so good for those suffering from anaemia. Coconut milk is high in fat and calories so should be consumed with moderation.

# Peanut Butter Smoothie

**Serves 1    Calories: 279**

## Ingredients

**1tbsp peanut butter**

**1 small fresh or frozen banana**

**150ml unsweetened almond milk**

**2 to 3 ice cubes**

## Making It

It is your choice whether you want to use crunchy or smooth peanut butter. If you can, try and go for the natural peanut butter with no added sugar – 1 go for 100% peanuts!

Add all the ingredients to your blender and blend for about 20 to 30 seconds or until smooth. If you prefer a thinner consistency add some water or more almond milk.

## Health Benefits

**Peanut butter** (when natural) is packed with the antioxidants manganese and niacin. Manganese is beneficial for bone strength, brain function and can have a positive effect on the mood.

# Orangey-Nana

**Serves 1    Calories: 275**

## Ingredients

**1 medium ripe banana (approx. 120g)**

**1 medium carrot (approx. 60g)**

**150ml of fresh orange juice**

**100g of fat free Greek yoghurt**

**2 to 3 ice cubes**

## Making It

Wash and chop the carrots and add all the ingredients to your blender. Blend for 20 to 30 seconds or until smooth. Add some water if you prefer a thinner smoothie.

# Ginger, Berries & Oats

**Serves 1    Calories: 224**

## Ingredients

**40g rolled oats**

**1 tsp fresh root ginger, grated**

**80g mixed berries (fresh or frozen)**

**100ml skimmed milk**

**2 to 3 ice cubes (optional)**

## Making It

If you are using fresh berries just pick what is in season. Otherwise, there is usually a mixed berries (or summer fruits) section in the frozen section. Add all the ingredients to your blender and whizz for 20 to 30 seconds or until smooth. Add some water if you require a thinner consistency.

## Health Benefits

**Oats** make another great breakfast smoothie. They contain high levels of soluble fibre that can help you feel fuller for longer, release energy more slowly as well as help to stabilise blood sugar levels. They are incredibly high in proteins and minerals.

# Banana & Mango

**Serves 1     Calories: 293**

## Ingredients

**80g chopped mango (fresh or frozen)**

**1 medium ripe banana (approx. 120g)**

**150ml orange juice**

**2 to 3 ice cubes**

## Making It

Peel and chop up the mango and banana (unless using frozen). Add all the fruit, orange juice and ice cubes (if required) to your blender. Blend for about 20 to 30 seconds or until smooth. If the consistency is too thick add some water and blend again.

## Health Benefits

**Bananas** may be higher in calories than other ingredients but they are well worth including in your diet. The high fibre content, as well as the high levels of potassium and vitamin C make them a beneficial addition. The potassium is a great energy booster – brilliant for including some exercise in your daily routine.

# Raspberry &Coconut

Serves 1    Calories: 238

## Ingredients

**1 medium ripe banana (approx. 120g)**

**100gfresh or frozen raspberries**

**150ml coconut water**

**2 or 3 ice cubes (optional)**

## Making It

Peel and chop the banana. Add all the ingredients to your blender and blend for 20 to 30 seconds or until smooth. Add a little water if a thinner consistency is required.

## Health Benefits

**Raspberries** are low in fat and calories yet high in dietary fibre and antioxidants.

The fat and calorie content of **coconut water** is very low. It is packed with nutrients including magnesium, calcium, potassium, sodium and phosphorus – the five essential electrolytes found in the human body.

# Tropical Brazilian Smoothie

**Serves 1    Calories: 280**

## Ingredients

**30g spinach**

**100g mango chunks**

**3 brazil nuts**

**150ml coconut water**

**2 or 3 ice cubes (optional)**

## Making It

Wash the spinach leaves. Peel and chop up the mango (unless using frozen). Put the spinach and coconut water in a blender and blend until smooth. Add the remaining ingredients and blend again. Top up with water if required.

## Health Benefits

**Brazil nuts** contain selenium, a powerful antioxidant essential for metabolism and helping the liver to work effectively. Selenium is required for maintaining skin elasticity and can relieve many symptoms of the menopause.

# Pineapple Smoothie

**Serves 1    Calories: 230**

## Ingredients

**100g frozen pineapple chunks**

**120g fat free Greek yoghurt**

**150ml coconut water**

## Making It

Add all the ingredients to your blender and blend for 20 to 30 seconds or until smooth. If you prefer a thinner smoothie add some water.

## Health Benefits

**Coconut water** has the benefits of being low in calories, completely natural, no fat or cholesterol and more potassium than a banana. Coconut water is a great way to hydrate.

**Pineapples** not only taste like a real treat they are also fantastic for supporting your immune system, aiding with digestion and eye health.

**Greek yoghurt** is high in probiotics, a healthy bacteria that helps your digestive tract by promoting a healthy gut.  By going for the fat free version you will be getting all the benefits without the extra calories.

# Cacao, Cashew & Raspberry Smoothie

**Serves 1    Calories: 263**

## Ingredients

**75g fresh or frozen raspberries**

**1tbsp cacao powder**

**25g raw cashew nuts**

**100ml skimmed milk**

**2 to 3 ice cubes (optional)**

## Making It

Add all the ingredients to your blender. Blend for 20 to 30 seconds or until smooth. If you are not using a high speed blender your smoothie might have a few unblended cashew bits in it. Add water if you require a thinner consistency.

## Health Benefits

**Raspberries** are rich in vitamin C, manganese, vitamin K and dietary fibre.

**Cacao powder** is less processed than normal chocolate bars and cocoa powder. Cacao is also very high in magnesium – essential for energy, maintaining bone and teeth strength as well as maintaining a healthy cardiovascular system.

**Cashew nuts** are rich in selenium and zinc. Selenium is a powerful antioxidant necessary for metabolism. Zinc is a powerful immune system booster and is thought to be important for mental alertness.

# Green Tea Smoothie

**Serves 1    Calories: 256**

## Ingredients

**30 seedless green grapes**

**40g spinach**

**½ ripe avocado (fresh or frozen)**

**1tbsp honey**

**150ml green tea (cooled)**

**2 to 3 ice cubes (optional)**

## Making It

Make the green tea and allow to cool. Wash the spinach and grapes. If you are using a fresh avocado make sure it is ripe by squeezing it gently (it will be slightly soft). Slice in half and scoop out the flesh. I tend to use frozen avocado halves now that I buy from the supermarket as it saves having to wait for an avocado to be perfectly ripe. Add all the ingredients to your blender and whizz for 20 to 30 seconds or until smooth. If you prefer a thinner smoothie, add more water.

## Health Benefits

**Green tea** has a wide range of antioxidants within it. Studies have shown that green tea can increase the burning of fat, especially when exercising.

# Red Grapefruit Smoothie

**Serves 1    Calories: 214**

## Ingredients

**1 small red grapefruit**

**1 kiwi**

**1tbsp flaxseed**

**40g spinach**

**150ml water**

**2 to 3 ice cubes**

## Making It

Peel the grapefruit and kiwi. Put the spinach and water in your blender and blend until smooth. Add the remaining ingredients and blend again. Add more water if required.

## Health Benefits

**Red grapefruit** contains more carotenoids than the white grapefruit variety. Carotenoids produce vitamin A in the body which is needed for the immune system to function healthily, as well as being good for maintaining healthy skin, bones and vision.

# Mango Lassi Smoothie

**Serves 1    Calories: 281**

## Ingredients

**150g mango chunks**

**200g 0% fat natural yoghurt**

**50ml water**

**1tbsp honey**

**2 to 3 ice cubes (optional)**

## Making It

Slice the mango and scoop out the flesh (unless using frozen). Add all the ingredients to your blender and blend until smooth. Top up with water if required.

## Health Benefits

**Mangoes** are great for strengthening the immune system as well as helping with skin and eye health. They also taste delicious!

# Grapefruit, Pineapple & Banana

**Serves 1    Calories: 266**

## Ingredients

**1 small red grapefruit**

**40g spinach**

**50g pineapple (fresh or frozen)**

**200g low fat natural yoghurt**

**2 or 3 ice cubes**

## Making It

Peel and segment the grapefruit. Wash the spinach. Add all the ingredients to your blender and blend for 20 to 30 seconds or until smooth. Add some water if you require a thinner consistency.

## Health Benefits

**Red grapefruit** contains more carotenoids than the white grapefruit variety. Carotenoids produce vitamin A in the body which is needed for the immune system to function healthily, as well as being good for maintaining healthy skin, bones and vision.

# Cherry & Raspberry Smoothie

**Serves 1    Calories: 267**

## Ingredients

**80g cherries, pitted**

**80g raspberries**

**100ml skimmed milk**

**200g fat free vanilla yoghurt**

**2 or 3 ice cubes (optional)**

## Making It

Put all the ingredients in your blender. Switch on and blend until smooth. Add some water if you prefer a thinner consistency.

## Health Benefits

**Cherries** are rich in antioxidants and nutrients. They have a high water content yet are low in calories. The fibre content helps with digestion.

# Sweet Apple Detox

**Serves 1    Calories: 260**

## Ingredients

**1 red apple (Gala or Red Delicious work well)**

**2 tbsps. apple cider vinegar**

**½ tsp ground cinnamon**

**½ tsp vanilla extract (optional)**

**1 tbsp. of honey**

**150ml water**

## Making It

Wash and chop the apples, removing the core. Add all the ingredients to your blender and blend until smooth. Add more water if needed.

# Thanks for Reading

I really hope that you have enjoyed the recipes in this book.

If you have found this book useful I would **really** appreciate it if you could spare a moment please to leave a review on Amazon.

It really inspires and encourages me to keep on creating books. If you have any suggestions or questions please do feel free to get in contact with me at liana@lianaskitchen.co.uk

If you have any smoothie recipe suggestions, I would love to hear from you too!

Happy blending.

Liana x

# OTHER TITLES

Are you interested in reading any other books by Liana Green?

The #1 bestselling **Nutri Ninja Recipe Book – 70 Smoothie Recipes for Weight Loss, Increased Energy and Improved Health** is available from Amazon UK, USA and other Amazon stores worldwide, as well as the other books in the same series.

Printed in Great Britain
by Amazon

15221294R00071